Geo Targeting

B. Vincent

Published by RWG Publishing, 2021.

GEO TARGETING

First edition. July 16, 2021.

Written by B. Vincent.

Also by B. Vincent

Affiliate Marketing
Affiliate Marketing
Affiliate Marketing

Standalone
Affiliate Recruiting
Business Layoffs & Firings
Business and Entrepreneur Guide
Business Remote Workforce
Career Transition
Project Management
Precision Targeting
Professional Development
Strategic Planning
Content Marketing
Imminent List Building
Getting Past GateKeepers
Banner Ads
Bookkeeping

Bridge Pages
Business Acquisition
Business Bogging
Marketing Automation
Better Meetings
Conversion Optimization
Creative Solutions
Employee Recruitment
Startup Capital
Employee Mentoring
Servant Leadership
Human Resources
Team Building
Freelancing
Funnel Building
Geo Targeting
Goal Setting

Table of Contents

Geo Targeting

Welcome to this seminar on geographic focusing on. In this course, we will cover how to build your scope with geo-designated promoting. This course is isolated into three modules. Module one covers fundamental exploration, module two tells the best way to geo-focus on Facebook, and module three covers do focusing with Google advertisements. When this course is finished, you'll realize how to viably utilize geographic focusing for your business. So right away, how about we plunge into the principal module.

Module One

Welcome to module one. In this module, our specialists will cover how to do primer examination for your geotargeting effort. So prepare to take a few notes, and how about we bounce directly in.

Okay, folks, how about we get into some great exploration to ensure that our geo-focusing on depends on, you know, great strong, solid, truth. Furthermore, similarly as with numerous things nowadays, our exploration will begin here with the all-powerful Google. We will take a gander two or three instances of things that you can research and ways that you can explore, they all sort of start with Google since that is the means by which you discover the data sets that we depend on, and we will begin with this one here. Suppose you have a wellbeing or wellness item, and you need to sort out kind of the topographical scene of wellbeing and wellness in the United States, you may go to a site like the US wellbeing guide, and wellbeing data.org which would bring you here.

Presently, this is a breakdown by districts of different wellbeing insights in the United States. We should see here we have death rates alright so passings and stuff how about we go for something somewhat more explicit. What about hazard factors? Furthermore, that is liquor, and how about we come here to, suppose, diabetes, analyzed. Alright, so these are individuals who have been affirmed to have diabetes, and have been determined to have it. Furthermore, first thing, you're ready to outwardly look, which I as you don't need to outwardly look, you could utilize a bookkeeping page or a data set, whatever makes you day. I like these guides, I attempted to exploit maps like this since I'm a visual individual.

Presently, how about we view. I could be rectified and thinking this is the reddest one on the guide. There's a couple other red ones here too. In any case, suppose that we have a type of a wellbeing related item intended to assist individuals with getting in shape become more solid individuals who were battling with diabetes specifically, or perhaps we're even in the drug space. Right, and we're explicitly searching for individuals with diabetes. That would be something that we need to target Starr County Texas has a predominance extent of 20.41%, which is twofold the normal for Texas and twofold the normal for the United States as you can see not too far off. So on the off chance that we planned to proceed to do some focusing on Facebook advertisements or on Google promotions. Indeed, we likely need to begin with this area.

Also, we should toss in a lot of these other red ones too. So this is extremely amazing as you can see just according to the wellbeing point of view up until now, and we may return and return to that one there, in one of the later modules where we'll be really doing some geographic focusing within Facebook and Google.

Furthermore, presently how about we continue onward to another here. US marriage and separation rates by state we have another visual guide here now there's a lot of information. In this outcome here this one by the way is from census.gov. This is genuine government information here. What's more, suppose we select separation here, and we can examine these details. The separation rate in the US is 7.7.

Furthermore, a portion of these states are somewhat higher than that. We should see North Carolina 8.6 Tennessee 9.1 that is quite high. Kentucky 10.5 Indiana 9.9 9.2 13.0 wow 8.4 10.8 12.1 in South Dakota.

9.3 and 9.6 10.1 pretty high there 9.6 I think the most elevated one was Arkansas 13.0. So probably the greatest specialty on the web. As you're mindful, turns out to be the relationship and dating space, right. What's more, you know, marriage mentoring and save your marriage sort of items, even in the data item space, will in general be quite pervasive in that specialty. What's more, in case you will do some focusing on and run a mission and attempt to pick the best spot to run a mission. It would appear that Arkansas is the place where you ought to focus with your advertisements, I mean gander at that, there's an immense market there for individuals who possibly need to save their marriage, approve or work on their relationship with their companion. Alright, so in case you're accomplishing something in that space again these are simply models. We should have another look here, this is one of my number one ones. This is a genuine guide of provinces dependent on family middle pay.

Middle family pay.

That is really incredible. Alright, you can really sort out what their most extravagant spots in the United States are and focus on those spots in case you're attempting to target individuals who have cash in the event that you have a high ticket offering, or you're offering perhaps abundance the board or monetary arranging, monetary exhortation.

Possibly you have something that is explicitly for prosperous individuals.

This could help you out a considerable amount, how about we simply go through a tad of stuff here in the North East since the North East is somewhat known for being quite rich.

So middle family wages 61k so the $507,000 in that general area in New Jersey Morris County.

110,000 They're in Hunterdon County and there's some rich individuals in New Jersey.

Okay, so on the off chance that you had some high ticket stuff or in the event that you were selling something that you realized you needed to target individuals who are extremely rich, you could utilize this guide here, and geo-focus within Facebook or within Google advertisements. These districts to kind of expand the odds that you will have your advertisements seen by somebody who turns out to be quite wealthy. Okay, and another model here is it doesn't all need to be, you know bookkeeping pages and guides and stuff.

There's a ton in the media too in reporting, you know, measurements, socioeconomics are well known things that articles are expounded on. OK, and they're typically essentially investigated, so Business Insider here has a, a normal family a mean family article where it positions this load of various neighborhoods now these are significantly more modest than the district maps. These resemble explicit named neighborhoods. See that normal family pay of $492,000 804 92897 that is really huge situated in the San Francisco Bay region Diablo plays home to Mount Diablo State Department and Pacific Coast and so on and so on So individuals who live around here, in view of the normal here, are probably going to be six-figure workers.

OK, that is much more designated all things considered than, you know, a district map. Both are valuable, it relies upon truly the thing you're attempting to sell and afterward, what sort of focusing on you're hoping to do. So dependent on looking around a smidgen here with Google, we've concocted some great sources a smart thought for the super-rich live where the very well-to-do live right down to the area and things like, and things like you know, marriage, separate from rates, and wellbeing related stuff like individuals determined to have diabetes. We should bring that data into the two or three modules, And take a gander at how we can geo-focus on those individuals with advertisements explicitly for them.

Module Two

Welcome to module two. In this module, our expert will show us how to geo-target on Facebook, so get ready to take some notes, and let's jump right in.

Alright so here we are inside of the Facebook Ads Manager, and we're about to create a new campaign. And for this one let's choose an objective, you've probably been through this process before awareness consideration conversion are the three categories we're going to go with traffic here okay.

Alright, let's head on down to the continue button here. Since we're just wanting to get straight into the geo-targeting.

And we're going to come over here to locations, and we're going to click Edit.

And we're going to get rid of the United States, okay.

And we want to get a little bit more specific here. Now, let's have a look at our data again, let's say, for the sake of this example that we have a health-related info product. Okay, maybe it's a diet and exercise course. So we want to target areas that have high levels of obesity, and one indicator of that might be diabetes diagnosis, right. And so let's come on down here and find that red hot, just blood red county that we found earlier, that was Starr County in Texas, A starr County. In Texas, let's come back to our ad manager, oops, actually when I come down here and we're going to see if we can do a County Search

Starr County Texas there we go went ahead and zoomed in for us.

Right, and that's it, that's the location that we're looking for right there at the south part of Texas. And as you can see potential reach in Starr county is 37,000 people, that's a good size audience if you want to target them. And let's see if we can find any more counties that are way up there in the error rate of diabetes diagnosis.

Let's see right here in Mississippi. We've got another blood red one 119.16 that's Holmes County. Let's go ahead and add that you can add as many locations as you want here on Facebook.

Holmes County oops spelling Holmes County in Mississippi.

That's what we're looking for. Okay, so we've got that, that's been added our potential audience size is now at 50,000, which is good.

And let's see if we can find another one around here.

Let's see Oglala, South Dakota, now. My concern here would be that the population size might not be huge, although that might be, if I recall correctly, no I don't think so. I was going to say that's the Black Hills, but I think the Black Hills. Well, it might be, we'll see. Let's see what this does to our population and we'll also figure out how good my Midwestern geography is. So let's double-check how to spell that real quick.

That was Oglala Lakota Oglala Lakota, let's add that to the chopping block here, Oglala Lakota.

Now that's not actually coming up so I wonder if the Lakota is part of a less official naming designation or naming convention. That's the right spot. That's definitely the right county, okay. So, we've got that one there, and it actually just dropped a pin there, and I wonder if that has something to do with the naming convention difference. In this case, who just dropped a geographic pin with a radius there. Which actually brings up a good point. We could theoretically just drop a pin anywhere on the map if we wanted to, assuming that you've got the data and the facts right about where you're dropping it right. Let's go ahead and delete this one since we've already got one here for the county.

So there's Oglala.

And that's actually it's, it looks like it dropped it on the town of Oglala, but that's fine that's also the county there, and you could increase or decrease your radius as much as you want in the situation. So that brought our audience reach up to $61,000 we could run an ad right now to these people, just based on their locations, and we would know that of that 61,000 and unusually high percentage of them have diabetes, which remember we're not just trying to get the people who actually have diabetes, who have been diagnosed with it. We're using that fact, as a potential indicator of a broader problem. Okay, a broader demographic reality, which is there's probably a lot of overweight people who would like to diet and exercise and lose weight in this area, even if they're not, you know, diagnosed with diabetes. Okay, so some of these things, these are little signals, right, that that, that are useful for indicating a broader trend or a broader demographic reality that you're going after. Okay, now with Facebook, this lesson that we're on right now is mainly about geographic targeting obviously but we could if we wanted to, get even further into this. So we've got people in these three really bad counties for diabetes which also means out of shape, counties, and we could add something like, people who are interested in Men's Fitness Muscle and Fitness magazine.

You know if you throw that on there, potential reach goes down quite a bit so you'd want to lose a lot of hand logic, by throwing in the fitness-related interests here.

So health, health magazine.

Alright, that brings us up to 23,000 people in those counties, that's almost half of the people. I can't remember what the number was before we started messing with it, but a very significant chunk of them seem to have an interest in health-related stuff. So, no surprise there. So we could keep going through here. You can click suggestions and just based on the ones you've already gone, it'll suggest a whole bunch of related ones health and wellness there, grow our audience by another 3000 Women's Health magazine stays about the same, Men's Health magazine, about the same.

The word work out, physical exercise brings us up to 37,000, physical fitness 40,000.

Weight training personal care.

CrossFit 40,000. So anyway, you get the idea you can just keep adding things all day long here to ensure that you've got people in those geographic areas who also have some type of interest in health, or filled fitness or wellness, which will help you with when you're targeting, right.

And of course, you could just pile on here as well if you've done your audience research really well outside of the geographic realm, and you know that you're also looking for people in a certain age range if you're want to if you're going to run a specific promotion to males versus females, you know, that kind of thing, it's all doable here, in this case, the core of it really is the geographic targeting, which is based on this, just incredibly, incredibly useful data here, visual data from a marketing perspective, I mean this is a marketer's dream come true right here, especially if you're in the health and wellness space. So now we're going to wrap up here and let's move over to the next module we're going to be looking at basically the same thing, but this time we'll be geo-targeting inside of the Google Ads suite. Okay, we'll be using that platform, and this time I think we're going to toy with the average income data that we looked at in the previous module, and we're going to try and track down and target some rich folks.

Module Three

Alright, welcome to module three. In this module, our experts will show us how to geo-targeted with Google ads, so get ready to take some notes, and let's jump right in.

Alright, so here we are we're going to start doing some income-based targeting, geographic targeting inside of the Google AdWords, or excuse me the Google ads platform as it's known today. And we're going to be looking for affluent people we're going to be trying to target some rich folk. So we're going to come over here to, website traffic, use as our campaign goal.

And we'll go with display advertising, we'll see that we have a display ad read we want to put in front of everybody in the geographic area that we target standard display campaign, and we're going to hit continue here.

Alright, and what we're going to do is right here at the top we've got location options already right. And then what we want to do is enter another location.

And let's have a look at what we're targeting here, and we'll see how we can target inside of Google ads whether we can do it by county or city or what.

And then after we've done that, we've got another cool little trick that we're going to have a look at as well. So let's try and find some more of these northeastern counties that we found.

So Hunterdon county 110,000 median household income from 2013 to 2017. So let's come over here, Hunterdon County.

And that was in I believe.

Let's see if I can find it again.

There we go, New Jersey, Hunterdon County, New Jersey, let's come over here. Let's start typing that in.

Hunterdon County New Jersey right smack there. Go ahead and go with target.

Okay, and over here you can see it's updating. So we can expect 59 million impressions. If we target just that one county.

And let's see here people in or who show interest in your targeted locations.

Let's say we want to get a little bit more strict, we want to say just people who are in or regularly in the target location itself, not just people who show an interest in it.

And let's see if we can add some more folks going by county, in a second, we'll actually bust out the map and get a little bit more specific, but let's just do a little bit more combing here.

Let's see here.

82,000 65,000 see if we can find something a little bit richer something stands out a little bit.

Nassau County in New York 105,000 Nassau County 105,000.

In New York.

And with that, as you can see the impressions have gone up quite a bit. And so we could just do it that way we can literally just add it to our list of targeted locations, county, after county, after county. We could go, we could target the entire US, but only the super-rich counties, you know, you come over here in the San Francisco area. Sure, we could find some pretty affluent counties here as well 104,000.

How about down here in the Monterey Bay area 80,000 106,000 they're in Santa Clara County.

So we just keep adding like this but I want to try something a little bit more fun. So let's go ahead and scrap these ones.

And we're going to go to Advanced Search.

And this time we're going to go by radius. And let's go ahead and find that town that literally a neighborhood of just affluent people with an average household a mean household income of $492,897. That's pretty significant there, let's find that actual neighborhood. And let's just literally hyper-target that neighborhood. So let's go ahead and type in Diablo, Diablo California. And there we are.

And let's go ahead and drop this thing as small as we can possibly get. Let's try maybe 10 miles.

And oops, actually, I'm going to have to go into pin mode to do that.

Let's remove that one and we'll just stick our pin right there, but this time, we've got it set to 10 miles, a 10-mile radius.

We'll go ahead and click target. And that's what we're targeting right now, that one neighborhood in Diablo. Now, the thing with Google targeting and the radius, being so large, these neighborhoods, you're going to have a whole lot of additional targeting outside of this neighborhood, I mean I guess this neighborhood is probably only you know, three or four square miles large. So targeting 10 miles, you're going to have a whole lot of excess around it, but again just like within the previous module we were looking at diabetes being an indicator of overall health issues, obesity, et cetera, et cetera.

It's kind of the same thing here when you're targeting these neighborhoods, and the county map reflects this reality as well.

It's kind of a thing that if we're targeting this neighborhood and this neighborhood is so affluent, the outlying neighborhoods around it are most likely not always, but most likely also going to be relatively affluent neighborhoods as well so we're not really hurt at all by having a 10-mile radius around the town, or the excuse me the neighborhood of Diablo is that kind of makes sense, but let's go ahead and get rid of it.

And let's get a little bit more.

Ninja crazy here.

Let's put a two-mile radius right around, Diablo.

Okay, let's zoom in there. Oop I wasn't quite up into the right enough there wasn't.

Let's see.

Stick that one there as a placeholder, remove that one, just like I can actually click right smack on the town. There we go.

Little bit clunky but we're getting the job. Okay, and finally we'll get rid of that one, and we're left with just a two-mile radius around Diablo, that is pretty darn powerful remember a very affluent neighborhood, you know, half a million dollar average household income there, that that's pretty powerful to be able to, you know, targets and put your ads in front of that hyper-specific of a location, and that's what you're doing here and then you would move on, obviously to the rest of your ad stuff and actually create the ad and upload your images, your responsive display and so on and so forth. And people in those areas that you, hyper-targeted geo-targeted are going to see those ads and guys there's fewer things about today's technology, and the advertising and marketing space that are more powerful, than the ability to geo-target interest targeting that's fun, you know, it's very interesting.

It's interesting to target interests on Facebook, it's cool to poke around there and find all that it is very powerful, no denying it. But this is just some crazy Orwellian futuristic stuff right here, being able to hyper-target all the way down to a tiny little neighborhood that has and because it has a half a million-dollar average income for your high ticket offers. So hopefully you guys could take that as well as the lessons from the previous modules. Now that we just had to utilize some geo-targeting in your own marketing and your own advertising.

Don't miss out!

Visit the website below and you can sign up to receive emails whenever B. Vincent publishes a new book. There's no charge and no obligation.

https://books2read.com/r/B-A-QWUO-UYMQB

BOOKS 2 READ

Connecting independent readers to independent writers.

Also by B. Vincent

Affiliate Marketing
Affiliate Marketing
Affiliate Marketing

Standalone
Affiliate Recruiting
Business Layoffs & Firings
Business and Entrepreneur Guide
Business Remote Workforce
Career Transition
Project Management
Precision Targeting
Professional Development
Strategic Planning
Content Marketing
Imminent List Building
Getting Past GateKeepers
Banner Ads
Bookkeeping

Bridge Pages
Business Acquisition
Business Bogging
Marketing Automation
Better Meetings
Conversion Optimization
Creative Solutions
Employee Recruitment
Startup Capital
Employee Mentoring
Servant Leadership
Human Resources
Team Building
Freelancing
Funnel Building
Geo Targeting
Goal Setting

About the Publisher

Accepting manuscripts in the most categories. We love to help people get their words available to the world.

Revival Waves of Glory focus is to provide more options to be published. We do traditional paperbacks, hardcovers, audio books and ebooks all over the world. A traditional royalty-based publisher that offers self-publishing options, Revival Waves provides a very author friendly and transparent publishing process, with President Bill Vincent involved in the full process of your book. Send us your manuscript and we will contact you as soon as possible.

Contact: Bill Vincent at rwgpublishing@yahoo.com www.rwgpublishing.com